Book of Days

Vaughan Pilikian

Book of Days

Book of Days
published in the United Kingdom in 2018
by Mica Press c/o Leslie Bell
47 Belle Vue Road, Wivenhoe, Colchester, Essex CO7 9LD

www.micapress.co.uk | books@micapress.co.uk

ISBN 978-1-869848-18-7

'May it be you' was first published in *The Frogmore Papers*.
'How the sun slipped away', 'Shadows of the earth',
'Blooms bursting in the dust' and 'Here you stand' were
first published in *Reliquiae*.

EARTHRISE
stammers
in the waiting void.

Let us raise our hands,
blot out the sun with the ball of a thumb.

It is the fever and the storm
raging within,
raging in the arch of the phosphorus,
that will orient us,
that will open a way
on the tangled
wormwood
path.

HERE LET ME SHOW YOU
the stone that burned,
that fused
in the chaos
when the world was young,
the stone I found,
the stone I took and set
fast in a cage,
fast in a ring,
close in my chest,
close in my fist:
the stone, burning,
spewed from the vent,
dropped in the garden,
breached by paradise,
dropped in the pit,
raked up
in the ashes of your eyes.

To the blackened one,
to the burned one,
to the one falling and falling,
to Icarus,
to the sun,
to all its ferocity has undone.

To the shackdenizens,
to the burnt house people,
to the mother
with the fatherless sons,
to any who does not make the best of things,
to any the settled world shuns.

To the ragpicker,
to the nothing ones,
to the outlaw without knife or gun,
to the beggar who counts
on fingerless hands,
whose reckoning will never be done.

To the heroes
who have torn off their trinkets,
who have slashed the skin of the drum:
to the mute brave ones descending
into the eye
of what they have done.

A NIGHT SNOW OF WILDFLOWERS
spangling the sward,
the twilight
diminishing,
diminishing:

you shake me
as mantle plumes
rise in silence
to shake cities
and bury them in the sand.

I HAVE LEFT A TRAIL
OF TEARS AND SECRETS,
never knowing why,
why this had to be the way.

Perhaps I left these things for you,
these devils in the dust,
but you will never find them,
never care for who I was.

There is one thing I know for sure,
one thing I can say:
were I to pass this way again,
I would do what I have done.

I would leave these things for no one,
burning in the traces,
seething still seething
in the desert of my faith.

How the sun slipped away,
how the wind
rattled the trees above us,
took the leaves off,
swirled them at our feet.
How the world seethed.

At junction of day
the alignment: three planets
and the waning moon,
a blade edged in gold,
its tranquillities
unenshadowed.

At junction of night,
silent and distant
the trees bend and writhe
beneath the hand of the wind.
How mysteriously fall the runes
of day into dusk into day.

I FOLLOW YOU.

I am leashed to a god
and I struggle to grasp
the fable you tell,

these words
plumbed in mummery,
the comedy struck from the cobbles,

the dazzling skybright clownwork
of your play.

IN A DAY
the wells are stopped with stones,
in a day
the orchards and the fields are turned over,
in a day
we are ripped from the land.

Here is the house
that never was,
the blind house, the house of silence:
unlock the door, throw the windows open,
sit for a time
in the sun.

Here scribed in ash is the book that burned,
the book that foretold
all to come.
Ash in its spine,
ash in its pages:
its pages are stacked
with the dead.

In a day
you are ripped from me,
in a day
love ends.
But my tears and your blood
turn to stones
to fall:

to fall, fall, fall
through all the days and the nights
of our children.

WHEN YOU
DRIFT
ASLEEP
it shatters my heart
again and again
and again.

I could cup your face
in one hand.

Your eyes hidden
in raptures,
you dive
into a forever
that will outreach me.

Your pain
and I not here
to clutch it from you.

Your dreaming fears
and I not here
to trap them.

Your sudden flight
all across
the stuttering lights
of my
ever
darkening
sky.

I AM TRYING TO GET ACROSS:
dark above and dark below,
I am trying to find a way through.
The rain comes down across me,
the wind strikes down across me,
across where I set my feet
and where I set my feet
the stones are sharp and fall away,
the dust is deep and fades away,
and I do not ask for guidance,
I did not venture for compass or map,
I would not challenge
what will not answer
so I sent out a line blindly,
out through hiss of rain
and thrum of wind:
dark before and dark after,
I am trying to find a way through.

WHAT CAN I DO TO HOLD YOU?
Do you hear me now
as you go below?
Do you hear me,
or are you gone?
Light as light,
how frail your arms
around my neck,
how frail my life without you.
O what can I do to hold you?
To hold off the world and time?
To hold off the ravening hellhounds
that strive among all I call mine?
Nothing dreams like we dream,
nothing falls silent or still
in the night:
the cries and the engines
go on, they go on,
the cries and the engines go on.
So I will stay while I can
and while you sleep
I will build us a shelter in song.

At night we went back,
we went back searching,
back to the caves,
to the veins in the dark,
back to the scree
where the dogs would run,
back to the hands,
back to the feet,
back to the limbs
of the swimmers in sand,
back to the lowering sky,
we went back to the disk
of the shattered sun,
back to where the killing stones lie.
We went back to the plain
where no living thing follows:
we entered
a vast black void.
We found ribs and skulls
glowing like moons:
these lyres and lutes
of our tomorrows.

IN FERVOUR.
In fervour I rise
with the stars,
with the stars and the blossoming trees,
to carry on the life that led to here,
the life that leads on beyond,
branching:
to stoop and stand and raise you,
branching,
to carry you,
branching,
if I still can,
if the need comes
and if it does not
then to fall in step and to go
beside you,
or fall in step
behind you,
past the perimeter
penning my dream,
past the fading dark paling to umber,
further, further and faster:
into the might of the day,
into the might
of hereafter.

TEACH US WHAT WE HAVE LOST:
how to listen, how to see,
how to give life through your fingertips
to the fox upon your knee.

Teach us how to meet the wind,
how to gather for a bed,
how to find in drifts of dead leaves
soft pillows for a heavy head.

Teach us twig by twig
how to lay the animal down:
teach us your wild lullabies
to sanctify the ground.

Teach us how we first drew breath,
teach us what we were made for.
Teach us what we were never taught:
how to animate, how to restore.

I REACH FOR YOU:
the desolated, the ones
whose legs are broken,
whose hands are broken,
who crawl,
who have wept and wept but now are done with weeping,
who go forth bentdouble,
who do not turn back,
who go and go and fall to rest
under broken rooves,
under broken eaves,
under the naked sky.

Look up
to the fevered dark,
to the ones who wander there and below.
Look o look and see them go:
white their hair,
black their eyes,
see how the rain has made them.
The cold encircles and binds and burns them,
and still they go,
they go.

I reach for you:
the destroyed, the ones
who rise,
who cast down their words and the words of others
who cast down themselves
and rise alone
blear and haggard, ragged and done,
into the harp of day.
O children of Aeolus,
you the elect,
carry the breath of our country.
To you I reach out my hands.

Shadows of the earth
upon the clouds
thrown by the unrisen sun,
the door framed in azure,
the gleam of the things
beneath my feet.

What carries us out
into the world
stirs within us
in blessing,
settles back upon us
returning.

The things that made me
are all undone
in the matchless barely there:
the vanishing light of the hour,
the vanishing
of the hour.

To the twain,
the surpassing wonder,
makers of light,
sky drops,
you who set your feet
so nimbly
between day and dusk,
who lend your hands
and raise me,
who lead me through the labyrinth,
bear with me
trapped in wakefulness,
let me watch you
fall away.
I take your hand and I take your hand
to lead you into sleep.
You trust me as your guide
but the two of you have brought me here.
You have shown me
how I lived:
how once I knew nothing of time,
and now
fond and foolish
in faith I follow you,
humbled
by the deeper world
you have somehow made your own,
ascending to the pinnacles
of your gleaming
empire,
a place I have never been,
the only to which
I belong.

WE WERE RAISED AND THROWN DOWN,
we were scorched in the gale,
we were cast from the height,
we were hammered in the hail.

We were longing, longing,
we were flayed with need,
we picked the sand from the rock,
we cut the soles from our feet.

We went lost in the night,
we went astray in the day,
we hobbled on our knees,
we filled our mouths with rain.

We have nothing, we are nothing,
we are gone, we are gone.

Now day, rising: engolden us.

YOUR BIRTH IS TWO RIVERS TWINING,
winding in the high hills,
veins in a land
whose name is lost,
carried in your shoulders,
deltoid, trapezius,
carried in the crest
joining arm to arm.

It is the cry of the blood
that was lost to the desert,
lost to the air,
to the merciless sky,
climbing, rising,
drifting, falling,
rising in the wells,
in the trees of your skull.

It is the shadowless noon
passed in the gardens,
passed in the green
of the faraway mountain,
passed and passing
behind your eyes,
flooding the plains
you cross with the moon.

It is the clutch in the jaw
that is all that remains
of the bindings made
to stop the children's tears.
It is the knot in the heart
in the crux of the chest
tied by time
to stop short the breath.

It is the shudder and twist
that make the frame,
that wake it, make it
move as it must:
carry o carry
the charts and the books
and the dreamings
placed in your trust.

Rain
COMES IN
through the walls of the chasm,
lights here,
the birds

turn over beneath it, spirits gone, and are laid
to rest in the heart
of the left-
alone traveller, the rag-
wrapped
usher of leaves,
the flutecarrier,
crosslegged
on the square cut stone,
dog familiar in his crossed arms,
open in his damage as a flower is open

to breath,
patient, turned from the snarl:
blessed he is blessed
in the falling
glow.

AND THIS FLICKERING,
this being hence, this nothingness,
this chaos, this panic,
these night fears,
this lying down not knowing who you are,
when you are or where,
and always the evening is too short,
always withholds
a thing undone
and always the night breaks in upon you,
its white beams
break over you,
and always the day comes too soon,
a fiery intruder,
harsh and unheralded:
and when at last you rise,
blearing and raw and alone again,
the questions of the night still hang like crows
in the ragged white dawn
snagged in the trees
above you.

WHEN TIME HAS TAKEN BACK ITS GIFT,
when I can go no further,
then carry me through
to the dark margin,
carry me over
the broken stile,
into the copse
where heads were hung,
into the village
where the bells fell to earth,
carry me past
the bristling fields,
carry me through
the battering hail,
carry me on
to where the sky was cut down,
carry me over
the hour of my ruin
and bring me in
to the lightless room,
the room with the roof blown in,
in the house
no longer standing,
and there sit with me a while:
let me watch the moonlight
fall
into the font of your hands.

It is
NOT ENOUGH, not enough
to be scattered, to be
riven and twisted,
to be split through, sundered, to be
thrown, thrown,
not enough to be lost, to be
blighted and torn,
to battle back, diced up, diced out, battle on:
not enough that
we gather and we gather and it goes and it goes
to the blade of the days, we are haze in the haze,
not enough
to be uncloven,
to have the skull whole,
to crave and to crave
the thick drug hidden
deep o deep in the gully of the night.
Break me, raise me, bruise me
lose me:
it is not, it is not
enough.

WITH YOUR EYES CLOSED
see the riverbird in flight,
see it turning in air:
it is perfect.

There is gold in your life
but it slips away:
hold it fast,
before the sun takes it.

THIS IS A LAND
WITHOUT LAND,
this is a place
burnt and glowing,
a place into which
I go and I go
by no means,
I go by no path,
I go without a way,
I go without hope
and without despair,
I go with nothing at my side
and with no one to guide me,
I go in with no way in
and no way through:
but I go, I go
with all that was and will
and can forever be
rising
like towers
on the moon.

Blooms bursting
in the dust
by the way.

A hand closed
on tears unwept,

amber in the eyes
like wolftracks,

a memory struck
and buried in the ground,

and low stars
pushed through the earth:
pushed through the dust
into day.

O BLOSSOMCARRIER
sprung from the sun.
O lifebringer
rising ever higher:
as you end in far future,
in my ashes,
blood pours from my eyes for you
and lifted on the returning curve
of impossible time
I will rise again
to find you again.

I give you
my all for all you
have given me.
Your eyes
and your voice
and your breath
glow and sing and blow through me:
branching through your tree
I live I know not when or how,
but I live,
leaved in gold.

Here you stand
at the broken staves
of the hour
that turns upon itself:

the polar sun has slung
its low ice beams
across your path,

the starlings
still
in the leafless trees

and nothing
but the long sussurus
of a distant day
still passing.

FULL
NIGHT
hissing
with cold.
Indigo ecliptic
and starfield opaque.

At zenith the moon
fell into the valley
and broke across my skull:
milk streamed from the house,
streamed across the land to the borders of the land.

You slept,
or tried to.
I shivered
and I fell.

Silver tides rolled in to bless the trouble in the breath.
As the rivers flowed upwards
something sang in the bones,
something fluttered,
something froze,

transfixed
by the millionyear momentum
of nightpulled
earthstrung
moon-
light.

HALOED SHADES,
neither breath nor clay,
pitched at forever
but bound to
the day: the day
brittle with gold,
played out
in the fingers of the wind.

We stay a while
to stay the time,
we steer the distance
to stay
the way: the way
that wavers
to hold us
we hope to bend
to make a coast
or shape a grove
to bind us,
to bear us in,
enfold us,
to bear us up,
glade us off,

to glade within us the day
that cracks
and flakes away
that breaks
and breaks
and blows away,
that flakes
and fades away.

LINGERING
I wait for you,
for the pale petals of your touch,
the amethyst in your shadow.
I wait,
and I wait.

Heartshudder
and the tired eyes:
faraway voices raised aloft
throng to the cyphers of the night.

I wait here.
I go down to my knees and here
I will remain.

May the moonlight
chalk my open hands,
mark them
with the passing hours,
with regolith
from the lost earth,
that nameless and forgotten twin
that burst
to share its glass and dust

to make bones,
to make veins,
to make the blood between them.

Faraway voices fading,
the first hour
falling past.
I linger here.
I wait for you.
I wait.

THINKING TO FIND YOU
drifting through walls,
out beyond the precipice edge,
stilled
by cease of sun pistons,
quieted
by miracle of day,
above abyss
wandering,
waiting at the spillways
of midnight past:

dreams of blood,
dreams of ruin,
rain smatters the wind
and my eyes,
and my eyes looking through,
looking out and in,
become twin dark mirrors
for you.
For I am the one: I do not dwell here.
I am the one that is far away.
I am the one that is gone.

THE ARROW
OF LONGING
flew and flew
and fell
and vanished in the valley
of my throat.

The streams of blood
spread through a silent land,
all unhearkening,
all stunned to dark.

I yield to the fall of day.
I yield to the faraway rain.
I yield to song
gone silent,
I yield, I yield
to you.

O to breathe,
to breathe.
Without you,
with you:

with you,
without you.

WHITE BIRD
you move
between living and dying,
higher and higher
on warm air rising:
your flight
sets the beat of the storm.

You surge and fall and glide and climb:
you carry all that we ask when we are lost to you,
lost to ourselves,
when we drift in the fever of time.

Higher and higher you go,
you go: a fleck,
a mote in immensity.
What is and what was and what will never be
can spangle the curve of your wings.

Your time is no longer
our time,
but your cry will presage
the sun.

To go as you move
ever before us
is to ride out the closing, the collapse, the shearing,
to swallow a fistful of feathers,
to find how sky and horizon fuse,
to circle back
within.

I suffered the day:
it came down,
it crashed down
over me, its struts
ripped up in the plumes of the vortex,

and when the eye opened
ink welled from the air
and enveloped me,
and dreaming
or dying
I fell into
its depth,
its tide plush and thick
and pillowing around me.

I was drunk by the mouth of forgotten night dark:
o love o love
I entered that hour
the fold of the lost.
I watched them
dimly,
sickled against fences,
I felt their warmth and their pride
as they bumped
blind and lightless
and gentle as sheep
beside me,

and I shared their gleam,
strung like bones
out across shadow and nothingness.

I HUNTED FOR A KIND OF SOLACE
that might be hidden behind the sun.

I hunted
through the collapsing day,
I hunted
through the trees of stone,
down all the avenues of eclipse
I hunted on, I hunted on,
I hunted through
to you.

To you,
pulled from the earth:
your delicate hands like roots.
Your grey eyes spoke
of damaged songbirds
pumping the cage of your chest

and they sung me across to you,
swung me down,
took me through the obliterated dusk,
until high above
the bleeding city
in your attic room
I strayed into a sulphur valley

while rain
fell softly
into the deep black waters
that rose and revelled
inside you.

THOSE THAT CARRY THE RHYTHM OF DAYS
are gone, gone
to the bright land.

They have left the play of shadows.
They have abandoned the ruined game.
They have taken with them
heaven and earth
and left nothing in their name.

So fill your hands
with nothing: bunch nothing
in your fists,
and turn yourself
against the world,
against the lies that made you,
against your own domain.

The trumpet
sounds at the splitline horizon,
the travelling star
dies
and the walls give way
behind you.

Before you
stand the candles,
the circle set at your birth,

waiting for you
to bring the spark
from the dusk and flare of your eyes.

WELL AFTER
THE SUN WENT DOWN
I saw you
meshed in flame,
flowing upwards in some high quiet room,
the air around you
split wide in the heat.

You turned over,
suspended perpendicular, rising an inch,
your head
bumping the wall,
your hips
twisting, lapped by fire,
your legs
bound in ropes of smoke,
your eyes

ice blue, untouched,
set deep
on some high tarn,
and they gleamed its cold cruel amaranthine light
back
through the hole
in my chest.

I KNOW YOU,
path through the dust.
I have seen this country before:
somewhere
it has lived in me.

Signed by the white ant,
purged of all birdsong,
blazed
then erased
in ochre and in ash:

I have followed you before
as surely as I breathe,
as surely as your butterflies
now draw me on,
on through the swelter of the day.

Pathway to the interior:
I can make no mark upon you.
I am a stranger here
and yet

I know you.
Impossibly
I have trudged before
beneath the gong of your sun,
on and on,

into your chaos,
into your white dust,
on
into your infinity.

SOMETHING HOWLED THROUGH US,
ripping up the air,
scattering it in tatters around us:
a single star shone,
trembled and shone,
the sky flared
and went out.

In time to come
the days to come
will blind us
and with cold coals for eyes,
fiercely,
we shall seek out hazard
in the dead zones of the night.

GASPING IN THE DARK
you reached out: you reached out
and threw back the bolts,
and fire rolled in like burning oil,
rolled on
into the kindled day,
rolled on into the smouldering dusk
and on
into the twisting bonedry forest
that made up the night for me,
that carried the fury
into me,
threw me down,
threw me over.

In sleepless hours,
in listless ways,
I tear myself in and out of rooms.
I wander the jagged upheaved streets
and my throat flares and
my hands, my hands
that once gathered you in
now clench and stutter blained and streaked with stars:
all that I come close to,
all that I touch,
all that I take within me
I burn away to nothing.
I burn away.
I burn.

SHADOW FEIGNED
and floating and panting
like foxes stole within.

One long evening,
rain blading the window,
we went feverblind
with open eyes.

Forever burst from your chest,
a font of stars
blinking and dying
and dying and blinking
and dying
to black
in the dark.

I dipped my fingers in Lethe and Styx:
I painted a sigil upon you,
consanguine
beneath, and cruciform.

You and I passed under and through,
blinking and dying and crying and dying
in the curve
of hollow
and hand.

INSIDE ME
THREE SUNS
uneclipse:
three blade arcs,
three slits,
all sablenightburning
to fever so sere
to thin time and touch
to vigil,
to star heat,
to course the anatomy
to blood up and splendour,
each hour match a candle,
three circles uncloven
and thrown into splinter
all looming unwoven
and one
to none
to prominence begun
and burning
and breaking and
burning.

YOU CAME UP
through the briars,
and up
through the holly,
up through the tangle of days.

Below spreads the rose
in the curving lane:
the thorns rise higher
than the stars.

How golden you were in the agony of tomorrow,
you
trapped back
at the glass,

trapped back at the stairhead
by the birthing room,

to dream of the passage
struck here and always
that leads
through wildblindness and rain,

that leads to the dark beach
and on to the neverland
and in
to the place
with no name.

SMASH THE EARTH,
uncircle its orbit,
uncircle
the turning
of time,
to candle my eye
through night space
and spear back
by occulted sun,
and then to stop or twist the wheel,
the broken circle we dream,
the horses that merciless gallop above us,
the engines that no one has seen,
and lastly to clutch the ashen light
spilled at the far side
of love.
Away, away, away from here.
Take us forever,
take us away.
Take us
into dust and song.

LIKE LEAVES FROM THE TREES
the years fell away.
Like dust from our sleep
the years fell away.
Like radiant dreams
the years fell away,
the years fell away,
the years fell away.

And what did you hold
as the years fell away?
And what did you see
as the years fell away?
And for what did you wish
as the years fell away,
as the years fell away,
as the years fell away?

Like cinders in bonfires
the years fell away.
Like songs in your heart
the years fell away.
Like your eyes from mine
the years fell away,
the years fell away,
the years fell away.

IN THE HEAT
OF THE LABYRINTH
I dropped a flower for you:
for you, for you,
for you.

It hissed and sputtered,
it flared as it fell,
it flared like snow into flame.

Fire in the heart
that burns upon itself,
that burns and burns
all the days that are gone,
that burns all the days to come.

In a maze of strife
and forgetting
I left behind a flower for you.

THE GIFT IS IN THE GIVEN
but what is given in the gift is
gone: it is gone
like the firefly
trapped in the hand,
gone
like the fork
fevered in the storm,
gone
like the words
whispered in the dream,
gone
like the bluebell
dying into summer,
gone, it is gone,
though the gift yet remains.

Take courage to find yourself
suddenly bereft:
grace upon you
is falling dust
that does not fall to earth.

To you,
set there
in the faraway.

To you and only to you.
To your white light,
to your dream well,
to your mystery.

Longed for,
longfaring,
longpassing,
long gone.

Belonging: deeply,
in all the vast and lonely byways
of the distant.

I FLEE: I flee
from burning nights
crammed with people I do not know,
people who beckon me back
to a place I left
long, long ago.

Now the sky
is full of gold,
dreamheated,
trees half in leaf
steeled darkly
against it.

It is not dawn nor is it dusk:
it is a time I do not know.
Like a bell cast
from the bronze of forgotten days
it calls me into itself
and I go.

Sleep now:
I saw you torn.
I saw your heart laid open,
to strive above the fretted shapes
of the night that never comes.
I saw your eyes
dim and strange
in the measureless orbits of loss.
So draw back your heart
and draw back your eyes,
draw them in
towards you,
draw them close and close them.
Leave the dark to the dark.
Sleep now
for a time.

RAGE O RAGE
of the going in the flicker:
the night passages
between glimmers,
the coils of sorcery
trapped in the hand,
the blood
turning to wild honey.

O my locusts and birds,
gemlike and dreaming
you will fly forth and feast
on what is left of me,
flutter and ride
so darkly bright
on the bluster
of the blossoming day.

SOON AFTER SUNDOWN
the gleam abrades the trees:
lustre in the path
and I thread my way to you.

Far past midnight
moonbeams ladder the earth:
the owls drop to dream
and I thread my way to you.

The dawn lost to the day,
the dew to the dandelion:
the hills go on forever
and I thread my way to you.

WHOEVER YOU MAY BE
come walk again
beside me,
walk in the dreams,
in the dreams where we met:
walk in the wilderness
where wordless
and wounded
you came forth to meet me,
where you went for a time
at my side.
You went for a time without word or whisper
and then you went on,
you went on
and away.
You found a way on,
a way into always,
and now bound somewhere
between never and forever,
outbound or inbound
or neither of these,
I walk up, I wake up, I walk out, I walk on:
I walk into the dreams
that bring you to me,
on and on,
always
and away,
on and always
away.

THE TWILIGHT SINGS
IN THE SHADOWS,
softly softly sings in the dark,
folds falling in waves
into me,
the last breaths of the day
settle deep
and the shimmer in the sky
rushes, breaks
and retessellates.

The day will come
when the day will come,
when the day will come to me,
when I will come
to the day,
come to the day's rays,
raised on the curved blades
drawn by the dying sun:
I will be raised on the rungs
of the sun.

And I will climb the ladder
that gives way beneath me,
gives way beneath,
gives way:
for the stars of the past
have been scattered through us,
hymnal the earth
gathers speed,
and the brightborn dark
falls faster.

You: you.
Who are you?
In my sleep
I turned and turned
the prayer wheel of your words.
I felt your hands on my heart,
I tried to touch what you had said.
I rose from my sleep
without you,
o stranger
I rose up alone.
I rose turning your words
and I heard a lonely bird
sing for you, sing for me,
sing for nobody.
Why did you come to me?
Where did you go?
Who are you?
Who are you?

I FELL AND I FELL
through the night:

high above
the dream continents,
desert
and crystal,

I felt gravity
bind within me.

Once long ago I set my hand to the edge
between blindness and silence.
It kindled,

and the hour and the hour to come
both were named,
both were promised us.

Now the light plummets with me
up
into indigo,

the dead
stir in their graves

and one by one
a thousand windows

fall open

in the sky.

O STRANGER IN THE DREAM
so familiar.
O walker
in the laneways of midnight.
Too far have you carried
your buckets of black sand,
too long have you yearned
for the well.
So set down your yoke,
pour out your burden:
pour out the mystery
of your life.
Let it hiss free,
sharp and glinting.
Let it fill the oasis between us.
I will not speak.
I will not approach.
I will not harm your peace.

BRIGHT TENEBRAE:
flicker with darkness.
Bright tenebrae,
young then old.
Bright tenebrae:
seized in the inbetween.
Bright tenebrae,
lost in the gold.

O TO BE
purely, purely
to be, to be,
purely to be.
Not to do or go
or sleep or wake
or struggle or strive
or dream or die
or wish or will
or build or break
or love or loathe
or wound or whisper
why, whisper, whisper why,
whisper, whisper why.
But to be,
breathe,
butterfly:
to be,
only to be.

Deep in the silence
of the night
I am woven,
I am unwoven.
I call out to you, I cry out.
A taper burning,
a braided flame,
a tangle,
a shower of sparks:
whatever I am frays away,
whatever I am
comes apart.
Deep in the night
and the silence
I cry out to you in the dark.

O WORLD
you filled me
with wonder,
with disbelief,
with belief.

And thus
I give myself back to you
now the dream
of me
is done.

MILK FROM THE KNEE,
honey of the eye,
bread broken
in the thumb:

may I carry what I have,
carry what I am,
carry what I need
to come home.

The prayer horns are blown:
the dark trumpets.

In the mighty dusk
we must
go to them.

Under earth, under the shadow of earth:
the horns.
Nightcrafted.

To hear them
fill with longing
as sails
fill with the wind.

We must go
to hear our longing:
the horns,

atombright,
chased
in saint and satyr,
moondrunk and suncupped,
blood tokens
stolen from the living,

the horns,
whose fashioning finished us.

Fathoms down and fathoms down,
a stairwell,
unwinding

and we
standing
and
listening.

Swallowed up
by breathsong.

Like hunters or players we carry the dusk
and its birds
inside us:
circling,

circling,
inside us.

Arrows of sleep
bowed from the sun.

Arrows loosed into twilight
arch overhead then break the dark
and cross deeper
like swallows,
like echo.

Slowly,
I fade.
I fade,
slowly.
The river
pours through the walls
and I roll into it.

I sink
into the swirl
dreaming of the neverlost,
longhorizonshining,
the meadows,
the meadows.

I dream of a word:
abounding.

MAY IT BE YOU
and none but you,
fluted
in plainsong,
shuttled in the blood,
carried in the heart,
bygone and still to be,
starblown and chrysalid,
fletched
in lazuli blue:
may it be you
and only you
who walks the stations
of the hours
of our days.

Index

Lightning Source UK Ltd.
Milton Keynes UK
UKHW02f0913240618
324664UK00009B/205/P